Resurrection: Myth or Fact?

Resurrection:
Myth or Fact?

by

Russell V. DeLong, Ph.D.

Beacon Hill Press of Kansas City
Kansas City, Missouri

First Printing, 1980

ISBN: 0-8341-0619-1

Printed in the
United States of America

FOREWORD

Were the following pages written only to convince gainsaying skeptics, its readership potential would indeed be limited. Nor is its purpose to bolster the faltering faith of halfhearted believers. Rather, its mission is to bring into focus the glorious truth of scripture in a delineation of "many infallible proofs" that Christ arose from the grave and lives today.

In a world motivated by materialism, dominated by self-interest, lulled to apathy and complacency in church circles, how vitally important it is that God's people be stirred to a vibrant faith, inspired by the compelling truth of the resurrection of our living Lord, "the same yesterday, and to day, and for ever."

The thought that one day we shall be like Him in resurrected glory invites us to forget temporary woes, disappointments, frustrations, and all other limitations inherent in our humanity.

Dr. DeLong's essay offers a tonic to all Christians; to read it is a lifting experience.

M. A. (Bud) Lunn

INTRODUCTION

It is a very strange fact, corroborated by ministers, that we very seldom hear a sermon on (1) heaven (except at a funeral service), (2) hell, or (3) the Resurrection, except on Easter Sunday morning when because of special Easter music the sermon on the Resurrection is limited to 10 or 15 minutes.

The Resurrection is the cardinal doctrine of the Christian religion. It is either true or false. It is either the most important doctrine because of its truth or the most fallacious of all Christian dogmas because of its error.

It is the purpose of this essay to examine, explore, and consider logically, step by step, the points which will lead to the belief in the Resurrection as valid.

One of the writer's unusual hobbies is to visit cemeteries, read epitaphs, and especially pay respect and homage to men who have made great contributions to human history. I have reverently removed my hat or knelt at the sepulchres of:

Napoleon Bonaparte, Victor Hugo, and Francois Voltaire in Paris;
William Shakespeare in Stratford-on-Avon;

John Knox in Edinburgh, Scotland;

William Pitt, David Livingstone, William Wilberforce, Isaac Newton, Lord Tennyson, Robert Browning, Thomas Hardy, Geoffrey Chaucer, George Frederick Handel, Charles Dickens, and Rudyard Kipling;

Mary, Queen of Scots, Queen Elizabeth I, and Oliver Cromwell;

Dag Hammarskjold;

Vladimir Lenin in Red Square, Joseph Stalin (first in Red Square and later removed from the mausoleum to the Wall). During my last visit to Moscow, I requested the guide to point out Stalin's grave. He ignored the request three times but finally, still very reluctant, took me to the spot at the base of the Kremlin Wall.

In London my sister and I spent the most of a cold, drizzly day riding busses to the cemetery where Karl Marx, the founder of Communism, is buried. After much difficulty we finally found the grave and noticed that vandals had defaced the small monument.

The first time we went to John Wesley's Chapel (we have been there several times since) was very thrilling. We entered the home of Wesley, sat in his study chair, knelt at his place of prayer, and visited other rooms. We then left the home and entered the famous chapel. I went up, stood behind the pulpit, and imagined John Wesley preaching.

(On our last visit to the chapel I had the unusual

experience of preaching from that high pulpit of John Wesley and conducting Communion for 248 faculty, students, trustees, and friends of John Wesley College from Owosso, Mich., where I was president of the college at that time.)

Then we went outside, walked to the back of the chapel and found the sepulchre of John Wesley and also the resting place of Adam Clarke and John Watson, eminent Methodist theologians. Across Avenue Road from the chapel is a small cemetery, poorly kept. Here we found the graves of Susanna Wesley, mother of John and Charles; John Bunyan; Daniel Defoe; and Isaac Watts, one of the greatest of Methodist hymn writers. In such an area and historical atmosphere I thought to myself what a wonderful place to be on the morning of the final resurrection as all these holy ones come out of their graves.

But the greatest experience of all came to me in Old Jerusalem. We went to the court of Pontius Pilate, tried to relive the trial scene, then trod the narrow, dirty Via Dolorosa (Way of Sorrow) out beyond the city wall to Mount Calvary. Here in our imagination we witnessed the Crucifixion scene and then walked to the Garden of the Tomb. The warden of the garden was an Episcopal minister. He showed us about the beautiful place. We plucked some flowers to bring home and then he said, "There it is! There is the tomb of Christ. Go in!"

I looked and observed a small opening. We stooped down and went into the sepulchre. In it were two small rooms which we inspected very carefully. The body of Jesus was not there. The tomb was empty. As we came out through the small entrance, the bells in my soul were ringing. *We had just visited the only empty tomb in all the world.*

The sepulchres of all the other great men to which we had paid homage contained their earthly, bodily remains. *Not the tomb of Jesus!* It was completely empty. The dead body was gone. Where? We believe that a dead Man came back to life. This we call the Resurrection.

But why do we believe?

The answer to this question is the purpose of this book. Let us consider it positively and logically, step by step.

Scripture Background:

Now the next day, that followed the day of preparation, the chief priests and Pharisees came together unto Pilate,

Saying, Sir, we remember that that deceiver said, while he was yet alive, After three days I will rise again.

Command therefore that the sepulchre be made sure until the third day, lest his disciples come by night, and steal him away, and say unto the people, He is risen from the dead: so the last error shall be worse than the first.

Pilate said unto them, Ye have a watch: go your way, make it as sure as you can.

So they went, and made the sepulchre sure, sealing the stone, and setting a watch.

In the end of the sabbath, as it began to dawn toward the first day of the week, came Mary Magdalene and the other Mary to see the sepulchre.

And, behold, there was a great earthquake: for the angel of the Lord descended from heaven, and came and rolled back the stone from the door, and sat upon it.

His countenance was like lightning, and his raiment white as snow:

And for fear of him the keepers did shake, and became as dead men.

And the angel answered and said unto the women, Fear not ye: for I know that ye seek Jesus, which was crucified.

He is not here: for he is risen, as he said. Come, see the place where the Lord lay.

And go quickly, and tell his disciples that he is risen from the dead; and, behold, he goeth before you into Galilee; there shall ye see him: lo, I have told you.

And they departed quickly from the sepulchre with fear and great joy; and did run to bring his disciples word (Matt. 27:62-66; 28:1-8).

Overall Text:
He is not here: for he is risen, as he said (Matt. 28:6).

WHY IS THE RESURRECTION SO IMPORTANT?

Because it does three things:

1. *The Resurrection validates Calvary.*
If Christ is lying dead in Joseph's new tomb, the Atonement on Mount Calvary is meaningless.

2. *The Resurrection guarantees Pentecost.*
If Jesus did not rise from the dead, He did not return to heaven, and thus He did not send the Holy Spirit to the disciples on the Day of Pentecost.

3. *The Resurrection makes eternal life possible.*
Jesus conquered our last enemy. Therefore death has no claim on a Christian. Death becomes merely a door from earth to heaven.

So the doctrines of Calvary, Pentecost, and immortality are validated and guaranteed by the Resurrection.

One understands, then, why it is so all-important that it be a proven fact. Therefore let us proceed to the irrefutable proofs that Jesus did rise from the dead on that first Easter morning.

In order to plug up any hole in our logic at the outset, let us assert that both sacred and secular history record both the life and death of Jesus Christ.

The fact that He lived is validated by history as convincingly as the truth that Socrates, Plato, Aristotle, Augustine, Alexander the Great, Napoleon, Martin Luther, Albert Einstein, George Washington, and Abraham Lincoln lived.

Also the death of Jesus by crucifixion is recorded by secular historians and is as factual as that Socrates died by drinking hemlock or that Abraham Lincoln was killed by an assassin.

So there is no argumentative conflict over the fact that Jesus actually did live and that He did die by crucifixion.

The only conflict is whether He arose again after having died on the Cross at the hands of Roman soldiers.

Hostile critics and disbelieving agnostics have created five proposed theories disputing the validity of the Resurrection. They know that if they can explode and invalidate the doctrine of the Resurrection, with one stroke they have destroyed the great superstructure of Christianity.

We are in agreement with them. Yes, if Christ has not risen, it is true that the doctrines concerning His deity, His atonement, His return to heaven, His promise of immortality, and His second return to earth are empty, false beliefs.

The five illogical theories constructed by wicked

men and conniving devils in order to undermine
the doctrine of the Resurrection are:

1. The Intentional Fraud Theory
2. The Swoon Theory
3. The Visionary Theory
4. The Telegram Theory
5. The Wrong Tomb Theory

It would be a waste of both time and space to explain these claims and attempt negatively to refute them. We shall not dignify these theories by explaining their claims.

Instead, it is our purpose in this essay to confine ourselves to a positive, logical presentation of the irrefutable proofs that Jesus did rise from the dead. When we have achieved this objective, the five theories listed above will have been completely destroyed.

We now come in our progression of thought to ask the first important question:

WHERE WAS THE DEAD BODY OF CHRIST?

See Matt. 27:57-61; Mark 15:43-47; and Luke 23:50-56. Especially note this record in Luke 23:55, concerning disposal of the body after the Crucifixion:

And the women also, which came with him from Galilee, followed after, and beheld the sepulchre, and how his body was laid (Luke 23:55).

Mark also corroborates Luke when he said:

> *Joseph of Arimathaea . . . went in boldly unto Pilate, and craved the body of Jesus. . . .*
>
> *. . . he [Pilate] gave the body to Joseph.*
>
> *And he bought fine linen, and took him down, and wrapped him in the linen, and laid him in a sepulchre which was hewn out of a rock, and rolled a stone unto the door of the sepulchre.*
>
> *And Mary Magdalene and Mary the mother of Joses beheld where he was laid* (Mark 15:43, 45-47).

In brief, following the Crucifixion, Joseph of Arimathaea, a rich man and counsellor, came to Pilate and requested that he be given the dead body of Christ in order to place it in his new sepulchre. Pilate consented and the body was placed in the tomb. It was witnessed by Mary Magdalene and Mary the mother of Joses. The Marys then left the sepulchre and went to prepare spices and ointments (Luke 23:56).

As noted, in the scriptures referred to above, especially from Matthew, the chief priests and Pharisees came to Pilate and said, "Sir, we remember that that deceiver [Jesus] said, while he was yet alive, After three days I will rise again" (Matt. 27:63; vv. 62-66 are given here).

> *Now the next day, that followed the day of preparation, the chief priests and Pharisees came together unto Pilate,*
>
> *Saying, Sir, we remember that that deceiver said, while he was yet alive, After three days I will rise again.*
>
> *Command therefore that the sepulchre be made sure until the third day, lest his disciples come by night, and*

steal him away, and say unto the people, He is risen from the dead: so the last error shall be worse than the first.

Pilate said unto them, Ye have a watch: go your way, make it as sure as ye can.

So they went, and made the sepulchre sure, sealing the stone, and setting a watch.

The evidence is clear—the Jews, Pilate, and the Roman soldiers had made the tomb as sure as they could so that the dead body could not be taken—it had been made safe from intruders, or vandals, or possible thieves.

Now, on the third day when the women went back to the tomb to anoint His dead body, it was gone. Nothing but the folded graveclothes and napkin was left in the tomb.

So the natural and logical question is: Where was the dead body of Christ?

As I have meditated and reasoned on this problem, I have reached the conclusion that there are only four possible answers. Let us consider each of them carefully and logically.

The Roman authorities hid it.

One suggested answer to this basic question about the dead body of Christ is that the Roman authorities took the body and placed it where neither the Jews nor the disciples could find it.

The logical question raised by this proposed answer is: Why would they do such a thing? If they had done so, the Jews would have been infuriated.

They had already told Pilate (Matt. 27:63) that "that deceiver said, while he was yet alive, After three days I will rise again."

Therefore if the Roman authorities took the dead body, thus making the tomb empty, the disciples would claim that Jesus had risen, "so the last error shall be worse than the first" (v. 64).

Furthermore, if the authorities took the dead body, not only would the Jews be furious, but the disciples also would be emotionally depressed, for they would not know where their loved one, the Lord, lay.

In the light of the above it does not seem logical to conclude that the Roman authorities took the dead body—impelled by no reason—and by so doing incurred the wrath of the Jews and aroused the despondent disciples. Historically, the Roman authorities did not antagonize the populace unless there was some major opposition to their rule at stake. In the case of the dead body of Christ there was absolutely no benefit that would accrue to the Roman authorities to take the body.

So we dismiss this possibility as an answer as to the absence of the dead body of Christ from the tomb.

The friends of Jesus—the disciples —took the body.

A second possibility as to what happened to the dead body of Christ is that the disciples of Jesus took the body.

There are three observations that should be made concerning this possibility.

First, the disciples had no desire for the dead body of their Master. Why should they take it? It was safer in Joseph's tomb than it would be anywhere else. Why move it?

Second, even if they had wanted the body (which they didn't), they had no power to take it after the sepulchre was sealed and secured.

Third, the disciples had no reason to take the dead body. Why would they have wanted to preserve a myth: that He had risen from the dead? Why would they lie about such a matter when they knew that He was dead and they themselves had the body? Why would they want to falsify to enhance their claim that He had risen?

There is nothing rational about the claim that the disciples took the dead body of Christ, so we dismiss it.

The enemies of Jesus—the Jews
—put it in a secret place.

If neither the Roman authorities nor the disciples took the dead body of Christ from Joseph's tomb, there is a third possibility, namely, that the Jews took the body and hid it so that neither the Roman authorities nor the apostles could find it.

Why would the Jews want to do such a thing? The body was well guarded; escape from the tomb was impossible; the disciples could not overpower the guard of Roman soldiers.

For the Jews to have taken the dead body of Christ would have been ridiculous. Why should they take it? And if they did, what place would they have buried it where it would be more secure than at Joseph's tomb? No! Everything was under control. They in reality had done as Pilate had commanded when he said, "Make it as sure as ye can."

But, just suppose that the Jews had taken the body. And here follows an unanswerable argument.

Peter preached his famous sermon on the Day of Pentecost that Jesus had risen from the dead. Here is part of what Peter said:

> *Ye men of Israel, hear these words; Jesus of Nazareth, a man approved of God among you by miracles and wonders and signs, which God did by him in the midst of you, as ye yourselves also know:*
>
> *Him, being delivered by the determinate counsel and foreknowledge of God, ye have taken, and by wicked hands have crucified and slain:*
>
> *Whom God hath raised up, having loosed the pains of death: . . .*
>
> *He seeing this before spake of the resurrection of Christ . . .*
>
> *This Jesus hath God raised up, whereof we all are witnesses (Acts 2:22-24, 31-32).*

If the Jews heard Peter—and they did—announce that Jesus had risen from the dead, why, if they had the dead body, did they not produce it and say to the people, "Peter is lying. He is not telling the truth.

Here is the dead body of Christ as taken from the Cross"?

They didn't produce the dead body. They didn't because they couldn't. Believe me, they would have if they could have!

If they could have, the doctrine of the Resurrection would have been completely obliterated. But as they did not have the body of Christ, they of course could not.

The only other possibility—Jesus did arise from the dead.

If the Roman authorities, the Jews, or the apostles didn't remove the dead body of Jesus, why was the tomb empty? There is only one other possible alternative—Jesus arose and came out on His own power.

All four writers of the Gospels report at length and in detail on the Crucifixion and the sepulchre of Joseph. The accounts concerning Joseph are found in Matt. 27:57-66; Mark 15:42-47; Luke 23:50-56; and John 19:38-42.

In order to carry out Pilate's instructions to "make it as sure as ye can," the Roman soldiers and the Jews went to the sepulchre and did three things:

● At the mouth of the tomb they rolled an immense stone too heavy for one person to roll back. Physical obstacle number one.

● On the stone they placed the Roman seal. To remove this seal meant death to any person breaking it. Governmental obstacle number two.

● To guard the tomb so that no person could go in or come out, they placed a regiment of Roman soldiers, possibly the best warriors the world has ever known. Military obstacle number three.

With all these precautions and guards, earth and hell, men and devils, Jews and Romans for three days and three nights rejoiced. The Jews jeered and mocked the disciples, saying, "There He is, the so-called Son of God—dead—incarcerated in the tomb. The danger to the Sanhedrin is gone; the threat of a new religion is past; the imposter is destroyed."

But as the sun arose on that first Easter morning, Jesus also arose, angels rolled back the stone, the Roman seal was shattered, the guard of Roman soldiers swooned as dead men, and Christ walked out in spite of the stone, in spite of the Roman seal, and in spite of the guard of soldiers, crying triumphantly, "I am he that liveth, and was dead; and, behold, I am alive for evermore, Amen; and have the keys of hell and of death" (Rev. 1:18).

Yes, Jesus came out having conquered earth, hell, and the grave. We no longer need to fear death and we have faith in immortality because He was triumphant.

In brief that's the great truth of the Resurrection. We believe that. But why? Is there reliable evidence? Is the Resurrection a fact or is it merely a pleasant myth? This question we shall consider and answer with irrefutable proofs in the concluding section of this essay.

Master Text:

And if Christ be not risen, then is our preaching vain, and your faith is also vain. . . .

And if Christ be not raised, your faith is vain; ye are yet in your sins (1 Cor. 15:14, 17).

TWO IRREFUTABLE PROOFS OF THE RESURRECTION

There is convincing proof from history.

Jesus called 12 men to be His apostles. They left their jobs (most of them were fishermen), their families, and their futures.

They were ostracized from their own religious background. They were hated, taunted, and opposed by the populace and by the Jewish hierarchy. They paid the price because they took up their cross to follow the One whom they believed to be the Messiah.

They saw Him perform many miracles—healing the sick, opening blind eyes, and even raising the dead. They loved and adored Him. No price was too great to pay for being one of His disciples.

The fact is they had trusted their lives to Him. They had gambled everything that He was the Son of God and would set up His earthly kingdom. They never doubted that He would overthrow Rome and upset the Jewish officialdom. So they followed Him and suffered what they thought would be temporary problems just prior to His victory in defeating Rome and ruling in Jerusalem.

After three years and six months two startling events happened. The treasurer of the disciples (really the first Church), Judas, betrayed the Master and committed suicide. Such an act upset them. Why not? If the treasurer of your church or business or professional organization had committed suicide, it would shock and upset you and cast a pall over your group for months.

I had such an experience. As a young man under 30 I became president of a college which was financially insolvent and in the hands of a receiver. We could not sign checks but had to requisition funds from the receiver's office to keep creditors from cashing in on our current funds. We began making an all-out campaign for gifts.

In the midst of this very trying and difficult situation I was invited to deliver the sermon at the annual watchnight service in our college town First Church. The chairman of the Board of Trustees and founder of the college lived across the street from the church. Both he and his wife attended the service. Following the sermon and the end of the service, sometime after midnight, Mrs. DeLong and I were invited to their home for our favorite drink—buttermilk—and an hour of fellowship. Mr. X seemed to be in good spirits and excellent mental condition, although he was aging.

The morning after New Year's Day the college opened following the Christmas holidays. At 8:50 Tuesday morning I picked up my books and proceeded to leave the office for my first-period class. The telephone rang, so I returned to my desk to receive the call. The wife of the pastor of First Church was on the other end of the line and in an agitated, almost hysterical voice said, "Dr. DeLong, I have terrible news!"

I responded, "What is it?"

And then in a high-pitched, agonizing voice she said, "My husband just went to our garage to get our car and take our daughter to college. When he opened the door, to his horror he saw Mr. X in his nightclothes hanging from a rafter by a rope. His body was dangling between our two cars."

I couldn't believe it, but I knew she wouldn't be fooling. It had to be the truth. I just sat in my chair —limp.

Mr. X had been a very prominent leader in the city and the state—former mayor, councilman, and member of the state legislature. He had a prosperous business. However, during the crash of 1929, he lost most of his wealth. Some claimed that it affected his mind, although I had never noticed it in my dealings with him. He had founded the college, loved it, and contributed much to it over the years.

I knew that the newspapers in our city and state would carry front-page headlines: "MR. X—A SUICIDE."

The college would suffer much. Students and

faculty would be distressed about it. Financial gifts would be difficult to secure. And I must confess I asked God why He would permit such a devastating tragedy. Here we were fighting to save the college, and to have this happen was a colossal shock. I admit it. I was depressed for weeks and somewhat discouraged.

The family of Mr. X thought they should plan a small funeral service in the chapel of the mortician. I advised against it, urging that we have the same type of service we would have arranged had he died normally.

The church was packed and hundreds could not get into the service; it was the largest crowd I have ever seen at such a service. Five hundred automobiles followed the hearse to the cemetery for the committal service. Mr. X was loved and admired by thousands of those who knew that his death was the result of a mental aberration.

A suicide—committed by the founder of the college and chairman of the Board of Trustees. Yes! I know what effect it had on me.

Well, what about the 11 remaining disciples following the suicide of Judas? It was a pathetic, unexpected tragedy. The man who handled their money was now lying at the base of a precipice with his bowels scattered all over the landscape.

What would they do? How would they respond? What effect would it have on them? Suppose you were one of the apostles. What effect would the suicide of Judas, your treasurer, have on you?

But as terrible as the suicide of Judas was, the bewildered disciples had a far greater tragedy—their Pastor had been murdered.

The suicide of Judas was enough to upset the disciples. The betrayal of Jesus and His subsequent death added to the mental anguish of the remaining Eleven. They had no idea Jesus would permit the Roman soldiers to crucify the One upon whom they had staked their all.

But He was dead. They had witnessed it. They had seen His "body . . . wrapped . . . in a clean linen cloth" (Matt. 27:59). They had been present when Joseph laid Jesus in his own tomb.

So in the space of a very few hours the disciples had experienced the suicide of their treasurer, Judas, and the murder of their Pastor, Jesus. Could any or have any human beings ever experienced such double tragedies of important colleagues in so short a time span? No wonder the Eleven were totally upset.

What was the next step? Here they were—11 discouraged, upset, sorrowing, wondering, questioning disciples. Their Leader was dead! The building of the Kingdom was at an end. All that was left for them was a final business session in the Upper Room before they returned to their previous vocations.

What happened in the Upper Room? There is no dialogue reported, but we can imagine something like this:

Peter arose and said, "I cannot understand what

has happened. I had no idea that Judas would betray Jesus. And for him to commit suicide is unbelievable.

"And I thought Jesus *was* the Messiah. I thought He *was* the Son of God. Remember when we were all down at Caesarea Philippi and Jesus asked us, 'Whom do men say that I am?'"

> *When Jesus came into the coasts of Caesarea Philippi, he asked his disciples, saying, Whom do men say that I the Son of man am?*
>
> *And they said, Some say that thou art John the Baptist: some, Elias; and others, Jeremias, or one of the prophets.*
>
> *He saith unto them, But whom say ye that I am?*
>
> *And Simon Peter answered and said, Thou art the Christ, the Son of the living God.*
>
> *And Jesus answered and said unto him, Blessed art thou, Simon Bar-jona: for flesh and blood hath not revealed it unto thee, but my Father which is in heaven* (Matt. 16:13-17; see Mark 8:27-30).

Peter concluded, "It is the morning of the third day. I wonder if He is alive and has really conquered death as He said He would."

Faith begins to mount in the hearts of the Eleven and hope resurges in their breasts. Maybe the suicide and the murder are not the end. Maybe Jesus is alive.

Brokenhearted John sobbingly said, "Oh, how I loved Him! I believed Him. I was sure that He would set up His temporal kingdom. I can't understand His crucifixion. He was murdered. I thought that He would call 10,000 of His angels and they would deliver Him from the Roman soldiers and the Jews. Now He is dead and buried in Joseph's tomb."

Thomas added, "Yes, I believed that He was a great Man—an inspired Teacher and a wise Philosopher. But I always doubted that He was the Son of God, and that He really was the Messiah."

Here were 11 downhearted, discouraged, sorrowing men on their way back to the old life. Their hopes had been dashed, their faith had been ruined, and their plans for the future were ended. Two terrible tragedies were staring them in the face—what could be worse?

They were just about to adjourn indefinitely when the door of the Upper Room flew open and in rushed Mary Magdalene, crying:

"They have taken away the Lord out of the sepulchre, and we know not where they have laid him" (John 20:2).

Following Mary's penetrating announcement, the 11 disciples sprang to their feet and rushed to the door. Hope had returned to their hearts! They rushed down the stairs leading from the Upper Room and headed for the sepulchre.

John, being the younger, arrived at the entrance to the tomb first. He had won the race. But poor, old Peter came puffing up to the tomb. He didn't hesitate but stooped down and went right into the tomb.

Peter therefore went forth, and that other disciple, and came to the sepulchre.

So they ran both together: and the other disciple did

outrun Peter, and came first to the sepulchre.

And he stooping down, and looking in, saw the linen clothes lying; yet went he not in.

Then cometh Simon Peter following him, and went into the sepulchre, and seeth the linen clothes lie,

And the napkin, that was about his head, not lying with the linen clothes, but wrapped together in a place by itself.

Then went in also that other disciple, which came first to the sepulchre, and he saw, and believed (John 20:3-8).

Here is a wonderful thing about Peter. He had forsaken his Lord at the court of Pontius Pilate. Three times he denied that he was a follower of Jesus, at least one time to a young woman.

Then took they him [Jesus], and led him, and brought him into the high priest's house. And Peter followed afar off.

And when they had kindled a fire in the midst of the hall, and were set down together, Peter sat down among them.

But a certain maid beheld him as he sat by the fire, and earnestly looked upon him, and said, This man was also with him.

And he denied him, saying, Woman, I know him not.

And after a little while another saw him, and said, Thou art also of them. And Peter said, Man, I am not.

And about the space of one hour after another confidently affirmed, saying, Of a truth this fellow also was with him: for he is a Galilaean.

And Peter said, Man, I know not what thou sayest (Luke 22:54-60).

But here Peter is now trying to find Jesus. In spite of his cowardice he wanted to see Jesus, confess his denials, and be pardoned. Peter loved Jesus. He wanted to atone for his cowardice. So Peter pressed right into the tomb (John 20:6) and also the other disciple, John (v. 8). Yes, the sepulchre was empty; only the "linen clothes" and the "napkin" remained. *Jesus was not there.*

So here were 11 men, wondering, questioning, and conjecturing about two tragedies—suicide and murder—and now they had seen an empty tomb. How could it be explained?

I imagine the Eleven wended their way back to their common meeting place, the Upper Room.

Thomas probably got the floor first and said, "I doubt that Jesus has risen from the dead. Probably the Roman soldiers have taken His body and hidden it."

Following Thomas, possibly John the Beloved arose and said something like this: "Oh, how I loved Him. Somehow I believe He has risen. Remember, Jesus said, 'And the third day I will arise again.' It is the morning of the third day. I believe that He has risen as He said."

Peter might have leaped to his feet and said, "Remember Jesus also said, 'Destroy this temple and I will rebuild it again in three days.'"

Jesus answered and said unto them, Destroy this temple, and in three days I will raise it up. . . .

But he spake of the temple of his body.

When therefore he was risen from the dead, his dis-

ciples remembered that he had said this unto them: and they believed the scripture, and the word which Jesus had said (John 2:19, 21-22).

There they were, 11 bewildered, wondering men. Their hopes had been dashed, their faith destroyed; they were on their way back to the old life—but then two things happened.

First, Mary Magdalene had been the first of the followers of the Lord Jesus to be privileged to see Him after He was risen. She came to the disciples with the glad news.

Second, the risen Christ appeared.

Climactic Text:

And as they thus spake, Jesus himself stood in the midst of them, and saith unto them, Peace be unto you (Luke 24:36).

What a moment! Here was a dead Man living. The 11 apostles saw Him. They heard Him speak. He heard them. Faith replaced doubt. Hope dispelled fear.

Even Thomas, the doubting one, seeing and feeling the nail scars in the hands and feet of Jesus, cried out, "It is He, my Lord and my God."

Then saith he [Jesus] to Thomas, Reach hither thy finger, and behold my hands; and reach hither thy

*hand, and thrust it into my side: and be not faithless,
but believing.*

*And Thomas answered and said unto him, My Lord
and my God* (John 20:27-28).

The resurrection of Jesus is witnessed to as a fact
by:

All four Gospels

Matt. 28:1-10. *He is not here: for he is risen* (v.
6).

Mark 16:1-7. *Ye seek Jesus of Nazareth, which
was crucified: he is risen; he is not here* (v. 6).
Luke 24:1-6. *He is not here, but is risen* (v. 6).
John 20:1-8. *She [Mary] . . . saw Jesus standing*
(v. 14).

All 11 apostles
The 70 disciples
Cephas
500 brethren
James
Paul

*And that he was buried, and that he rose again the
third day according to the scriptures:*

And that he was seen of Cephas, then of the twelve:

*After that, he was seen of above five hundred breth-
ren at once . . .*

*After that, he was seen of James; then of all the
apostles.*

And last of all he was seen of me [Paul] . . . (1 Cor.
15:4-8).

In brief and in summary, Jesus, after His crucifixion, death, and burial in Joseph's new tomb, was
seen by Mary Magdalene, Mary the mother of Joses,

Peter (Cephas), John, the other 9 apostles, the 70 disciples, over 500 brethren, James, and Paul.

They could not all have been wrong. They were not merely supporting a myth. They actually saw a dead Man living. Therefore the doctrine of the Resurrection became the foundation of their preaching. And the main objective of the apostles was to introduce non-Christians to the *living* Jesus.

The historical argument for the Resurrection is climaxed and corroborated by these facts.

The apostles preached the Resurrection everywhere they went. They could not be stopped. They were threatened, beaten, put in jail, and tortured. It did no good. They had seen the risen Christ. They feared neither men nor prison.

Ten of the 11 apostles died as martyrs. One doesn't sacrifice his life for a meaningless myth. They feared neither pain nor death. Why? Because they had seen a dead Man live. Jesus conquered death. So if they too would be killed, Jesus had the power over death and would raise them up.

How else can you explain this fact: Within a few days here were 11 men who were:

Discouraged

Despondent

Sad

and on their way back to their old life, when all of a sudden they became the

Most Courageous

Most Convinced

Most Dynamic

Most Radiant
Most Victorious
men in human history?
What changed them?

There is only one answer—they had in reality met One who had been dead but who was now alive.

There is no other possible explanation. People don't die for known myths. They don't give up their lives for false causes. They don't become martyrs for an illogical, unreasonable, fallacious belief. No! These 11 had seen a Man die, and now they had seen Him live again.

How can anyone explain the activities and exploits of the Early Church?

The Resurrection!

How could someone account for the enduring, triumphant Christian religion for nearly 2,000 years although attacked by skeptics, atheists, agnostics, higher critics, irreligionists, and other religions?

The Resurrection!

How does one explain that today there are many millions of members of Christian churches? And from A.D. 33 to 1980 there have been untold millions of followers of Christ.

The Resurrection!

Belief in the Resurrection is:
Irrefutable
Unanswerable
Incontrovertible
Indisputable.
It is a fact, not a myth.

There is confirming proof from personal experience.

The historical proof of the Resurrection is important, but the most satisfying and convincing proof is personal. You too can meet the risen Jesus.

Sinners by the millions have met Him. Thieves, liars, drunkards, harlots, dope fiends, and immoral men have been changed. New life has come to their souls which were "dead in trespasses and sins." Innumerable people have been transformed by the living Christ.

All men are sinners. All need forgiveness. All need pardon. All need to be "born again."

In the third chapter of the Gospel of John is recorded the confrontation Jesus had with Nicodemus, a ruler of the Jews. He was a moral man who had kept the Ten Commandments. But he needed something more. Here is what Jesus said to him: *Verily, verily, I say unto thee, Except a man be born again, he cannot see the kingdom of God* (v. 3).

He reiterated: *I say unto thee, Except a man be born of water and of the Spirit, he cannot enter into the kingdom of God* (v. 5).

And then Jesus added: *Marvel not that I said unto thee, Ye must be born again* (v. 7).

With these introductory verses John leads up to the most famous verse in the Bible—the 16th: *For*

God so loved the world, that he gave his only be-gotten Son, that whosoever believeth in him should not perish, but have everlasting life.

It is this personal, transforming power of the living Christ that is the final and most convincing proof of the Resurrection.

Permit me now to paraphrase the words of Paul and say, "I too met the risen Lord."

I was born and reared in a Christian home. My father was a minister. His salary was very small. To assist the family financially my mother always had two to six roomers and boarders living in our house. She worked hard without benefit of a washing machine or electric stove or other modern conveniences. We attended church regularly: Sunday four times (Sunday school, morning worship, young people's service, and evening evangelistic service), Tuesday night class meeting, Thursday evening prayer meeting; and during revivals, we even went every night.

When I was 16, a high school senior, I got away from the Lord and was hurting my father's ministry and breaking my mother's heart. No matter what time I came in at night, I would always find my mother kneeling at a parlor chair praying for somebody (me). This bothered me and upset me no end.

Finally, one Sunday evening I was sitting in the back seat in the church with my boyfriend. When the sermon was completed, I left my seat and walked down the center aisle to the altar, followed by my chum. We both confessed our sins and asked forgiveness. Something happened to me that completely transformed my life. I met the risen Savior. He forgave my sins and imparted His life into my dead soul.

That experience for me was the greatest proof of the Resurrection.

Grand Finale Text:

If there be no resurrection of the dead, then is Christ not risen. . . .

For if the dead rise not, then is not Christ raised (1 Cor. 15:13, 16).

THE RESURRECTION TRIUMPH

The triumph of it all: The Resurrection conquered death; so we too shall live beyond the grave.

The Resurrection is the great doctrine.

1. It validates Calvary—the Atonement.

2. It guarantees Pentecost—the sending of the Holy Spirit.

3. It provides immortality—life beyond death.

Jesus is Prophet, Priest, and King. In His life on earth in the past, He was a Prophet. Today He is the Great High Priest interceding for us with the Father.

In the future He will be the King of Kings, coming with more than 100 million of His saints to take His Bride to the marriage supper of the Lamb.

In my teens the dime novel—sometimes referred to as the "yellow-backed novel"—was comparable today with hair-raising radio and television dramas.

All such stories had three main characters: 1) The hero who was described as a strong, muscular, athletic type and with whom female readers would fall in love; 2) A heroine, beautiful of face and figure that young men would admire and want to marry; 3) The villain, a debonair, tall, thin, peaked-nose, suave individual with his hair plastered down and parted in the middle.

One night I sneaked one of those yellow-backed novels into my room which was in the attic of our parsonage. If my father had found me with it, I wouldn't have been able to sit down for a week.

I went to bed early in order to read the forbidden novel. It was exciting! The villain overcame the hero, bound him hand and foot, and dragged him out on the porch while the heroine cried and screamed. I could have killed him. My heart was palpitating and my interest in the action was at the highest peak. What would happen next?

Just at this climactic moment, my mother hollered up the stairs saying, "Russell, put your light out and go to sleep."

But I had to know the finish. I couldn't go to sleep and leave the hero suffering and the heroine screaming. So I quickly turned to the end of the book. Around the bend of the road came the sheriff and his posse. They galloped up to the house where the hero was bound, the heroine was screaming, and the villain was threatening. The sheriff overcame the villain and took him off to jail. I went quietly to sleep.

The next night I wondered what had happened between the time the villain had bound the hero and the arrival of the sheriff.

So I found the place in the book when Mother had called and began to read. The villain was brandishing his revolver over the head of the hero and saying to the heroine, "I'm going to kill your boyfriend, and you and I are going to live happily ever after." The hero was lying bound and the heroine was crying and screaming hysterically.

I said, "Listen," to the bound man, "don't be scared! He's not going to kill you. I know how it's all coming out."

And to the heroine I said, "Listen, young woman! Stop crying! Dry your tears! The villain's not going to kill your boyfriend and he's not going to run off with you. I know how it's all coming out."

Then I yelled to the villain, "Look, you criminal. You're not going to kill the hero and you're not going to take the heroine. I know how it's all coming out. The sheriff will be here soon; the bound hero will be liberated; the young woman will stop her tears; and you will be incarcerated in the state penitentiary."

The application of the story is this. We are all

living in a sinful world, suffering various degrees of pain; we are tempted by the devil and opposed by wicked men. Be not alarmed, be not afraid, do not despair, do not be despondent, do not be discouraged—it will not be long until Jesus, the Great Sheriff of the skies, the King of Kings, will come swooping through the heavens with "ten thousand times ten thousand" of His holy saints, to take His Bride to a city where pain and suffering and temptation never come.

The Resurrection makes such immortality and eternal life possible. Jesus conquered death, hell, and the grave.

CONCLUSION

The prospect of immortality is the greatest hope of every Christian. Eternal life is the greatest result of the Resurrection. The King of Kings is coming, and we are going.

Recently I reread the amazing account of the life of Dr. Frank Carpenter. He was born in the hills of North Carolina. Frank was 1 of 12 children. His parents were very poor and had difficulty providing the necessary food, shelter, and clothing for such a large family. Frank did not own a pair of shoes until he was in high school. He had a very good mind with a high I.Q. His teachers and friends thought that he must go to college. He applied and was accepted. He had to work his entire way through. His intellectual ability enabled him to become the valedictorian of his class. During his college years he had developed a desire to become a medical doctor. So he applied to a college of medicine and due to his high grades was accepted. Here again he was selected as the valedictorian. Several internships were offered to him; and when he had completed all medical requirements, he was approached by many doctors who offered him a large salary to become affiliated with them.

Frank considered these lucrative offers but made the decision to return to his hometown and county in order to serve his own people. He rented a room at the county seat, his home, on the second story of a downtown wooden building. He secured a piece of wood about two feet long and one foot wide. With a brush and paint he printed on the board "FRANK CARPENTER, M.D." Under his name he added "Upstairs" and made a long, pointed arrow. Then he nailed the piece of board to the wooden building on a slant so that prospective patients would know where his office was located.

For more than 40 years Dr. Frank Carpenter served his people. He brought hundreds of children into the world. During epidemics he tirelessly served at all hours of the day or night. He was greatly loved and highly respected.

Then one day he became ill. He grew weaker and weaker and finally crossed the boundary line between worlds. Sorrow and sadness filled the hearts of thousands of the residents of his county.

The day of the funeral arrived and so many people came that no church could accommodate the crowd. The ministers took the service to the cemetery. Following the ceremony the casket was lowered into the grave and the dirt filled in. As the people were about to leave this spot where their beloved doctor now lay, a man spoke up and said, "Don't leave! There should be a marker on this spot. Wait!"

Within a few minutes he returned with a 2 x 4

stick about 10 feet long, and on one end he had nailed an old, weather-beaten piece of board. He pushed the 2 x 4 in the soft dirt and on the top the people read:

FRANK CARPENTER, M.D.
Upstairs

Because of the Resurrection, friends at one's passing may read "JOHN JONES" or "PAUL BROWN" or "RUSSELL V. DeLONG"—"Upstairs."

A FINAL QUESTION

You have now read this book entitled *Resurrection: Myth or Fact?* The greatest personal proof is that you for yourself can meet the risen Christ and hear Him say, "Peace be unto you." Why not—this moment—confess your sins and accept Jesus as Savior and let eternal Resurrection life come to your soul?